Ocean
Animals

by **Sharon Gordon**

Reading Consultant: Nanci R. Vargus, Ed.D.

Marshall Cavendish
Benchmark
New York

Picture Words

 dolphins

 jellyfish

 lobster

 octopus

sea horse

 sea turtle

 water

 whale

3

Ocean animals move
in the ⬛.

The ☘☘☘ float.

The 🐙 swims.

The jumps.

The hides.

The glides.

The crawls.

The play.

I move in the ,
too!

Words to Know

crawl (krawl)
to move close to the ground

float (floht)
to rest or move in the water
or in the air.

glide to move smoothly

Find Out More

Books

Gunzi, Christiane. *Under the Sea*. Hauppauge, NY: Barron's Educational Series, 2006.

Rau, Dana Meachen. *The Whale in the Water*. New York: Marshall Cavendish Benchmark, 2007.

Stierle, Cynthia and Annie Crawley. *Ocean Life from A to Z*. Pleasantville, NY: Reader's Digest Children's Books, 2007.

DVDs

Dorling Kindersley. *Eyewitness: Fish*. DK Eyewitness, 2007.

National Geographic. *Really Wild Animals: Deep Sea Dive*. National Geographic Video, 2005.

Web Sites

Marine Life Learning Center: Kid's Corner
www.fishid.com/facts.htm

National Aquarium in Baltimore
www.aqua.org

SeaWorld: Animals
www.seaworld.org/animal-info

About the Author

Sharon Gordon is an author, editor, and advertising copywriter. She is a graduate of Montclair State University in New Jersey and has written more than 100 children's books, many for Marshall Cavendish, including works of fiction, nonfiction, and cultural history. Along with her family, she enjoys exploring the plant and animal wildlife of the Outer Banks of North Carolina.

About the Reading Consultant

Nanci R. Vargus, Ed.D., wants all children to enjoy reading. She used to teach first grade. Now she works at the University of Indianapolis. Nanci helps young people become teachers. She has been swimming with sea turtles in Barbados.

Marshall Cavendish Benchmark
99 White Plains Road
Tarrytown, NY 10591-5502
www.marshallcavendish.us

All Internet addresses were correct at the time of printing.

Library of Congress Cataloging-in-Publication Data
Gordon, Sharon.
Ocean animals / by Sharon Gordon.
        p. cm. — (Benchmark Rebus. Animals in the wild)
Summary: "Easy to read text with rebuses explores animals that live in the ocean"—Provided by publisher.
Includes bibliographical references.
ISBN 978-0-7614-2903-6
Marine animals—Juvenile literature. I. Title.
QL122.2.G67 2008
591.77—dc22
        2007042933

Editor: Christine Florie
Publisher: Michelle Bisson
Art Director: Anahid Hamparian
Series Designer: Virginia Pope

Photo research by Connie Gardner

Rebus images, with the exception of jellyfish, provided courtesy of *Dorling Kindersley.*

Cover photo by Eureka Slide/Super Stock

The photographs in this book are used with permission and through the courtesy of:
Pacific Stock/Super Stock, p. 2 (jellyfish); *Minden Pictures:* p. 5 Chris Newbert; p. 13 Fred Bavendam; p. 19 Todd Pusser/npl; *Corbis:* p. 7 Stefano Amantini; p. 9 Stuart Westmorland; *Super Stock:* pp. 11, 15 age footstock; p. 21 Pacific Stock; *Peter Arnold Inc:* p. 17 M. Mavrikakis.

Printed in Malaysia
1 3 5 6 4 2